RISE LIKE THE PHOENIX

Thomas S. Connelly

Christine Crane

Edward W. DiDonato

Kate Knetzger

Sean O'Donnell

Gregory D. Snyder, MD

CONTENTS

INTRODUCTION

By Thomas S. Connelly

This book is a collaboration among some old friends along with some new ones and its intended readership are people who have recently suffered some form of life-changing accident or medical and health challenge.

There are a few things we all have in common, the first being that each of us has experienced a major life-altering event, possibly not unlike yours. Another is that we all have, in one way or another, risen from those ashes like the Phoenix as in the title of this book. Now our purpose is not to share more down stories with you as if someone else's woes might be equal to or maybe even worse than your own and that that somehow is going to make you feel better. Nor are we interested in giving ourselves any special acknowledgement for our respective recoveries. Instead, it is our wish that if just one thought in this book provides you with the hope, the clarity, and the motivation to get back on track to the best of your new ability, then it will be a successful venture for us.

Now some of us had the good fortune to have a great family and friends' network to support us through those very confusing, questionable, and dark days. Others may not have been so lucky but with or without that support, it sooner or later boils down to just who you are, and what are YOU now going to do with YOUR new life? All of us have been there. All of us are most grateful for whatever support we got from family, friends, and certainly from the medical professionals who have cared for us so well, but we all also, humbly, have to state that a big reason why we are where we are now and who we are in life today, is due in a large part to our own attitude and determination. In one of the stories, there is a comment about everyone having an on/off switch. You need to find your own ON switch and while just flipping it back ON is an accomplishment in itself given your health reversal, just back "ON" is not enough since you are now restarting your life as it is today much further back in life's game from where you were prior to your life altering change. No, after you mentally find that ON switch, then to the best of your ability, you need to hit it with all the power and determination you can muster.

In sharing our own stories, the reality of dark times comes up, more than once. You will have your own dark times and it is important for you to view them as strength motivators; maybe for physical improvement but more importantly for your spirit and determination.

One shared example was being alone, at night, all visitors, family, and friends are gone. It is a very lonely time and you are left with your own thoughts and wondering just what the hell you are going to do with your life. How are you going to manage yourself, how much of a burden will you be to others? What kind of job can you get, even if you can get a job? How will you be able to live and where will the support money come from?

What is the best you can expect, and is all the work, time, and effort worth it?

Another added the fear he felt when the therapist said she was taking him outside to a public park the next day. He was so deep into and felt so secure in his foxhole at the rehab clinic that he had an almost panic attack about being seen in public. There is never a good time for a health or well-being setback but how about a major stroke just several days after giving birth? Again, you will have your own dark times, unfortunately maybe even multiple times, but it is essential for you to not give up. It is hard, and it is painful, and yes it is lonely, but hope and upward movement is coming. Your medical professionals will help you "bounce" back up but the degree of and the height of that bounce is up to you and only you. Find and work hard with determination on your bounce!

We hope our own experiences and "bounce" successes will in some way help you along your journey.

"CEILINGS"

By Sean O'Donnell

'm awake. I have a tube up my nose and down my throat that both feeds me and empties my stomach when needed. Green-brown bile trickles out of me. Another tube presses into my mouth and windpipe. It's doing my breathing for me. My mouth feels like a cold desert and the only relief is the tiny ice chips some stranger uses to wet my lips. The tube between my 4th and 5th left rib drains fluid out of my chest and reflates my lung. I am as desperate for a full breath of oxygen in my chest as I am for a drop of water on my mouth. My left arm is a purple color I've never seen before from a massive bruise that extends from my shoulder to forearm. It is too weak to move, and when I try, the pain it exerts on my system leaves me in agony. It must be broken. My right arm is strapped to the bed to prevent me from pulling the tubes keeping me alive from my body. I vaguely remember trying to do just that in between the unconsciousness and the morphine daze. The warm fluid running out of that tube onto my upper body from that action actually felt somewhat relieving in contrast to the cold dryness of the air in the ICU.

Everything hurts. Everything I can feel, that is. As I look down, my belly button is cut and resewn with another tube draining fluid there. I think, "That looks like it really hurts." It's starting to click, "Wait … why doesn't that hurt?" Everything hurts: every tube, every needle, my head, my arms … why not the lower tubes? "What's going on?" I start to panic; I try to kick. I want to jump out of this bed, yank everything out of me and scream. Nothing happens. Nothing moves and I'm more scared than I've ever been. Tears sting my eyes and panic sets my heart monitor off like a jack in the box.

This alert brings a rush of people who try calming me down. "Sean," they say, "you were in a terrible accident a few days ago. Try to stay calm. We are taking care of you." That's the first time I could remember breaking … it won't be the last …. This won't be easy.

Many moments try to break you when you go through something like this. Some people choose to give up, but at 17 years old, I didn't know that I had a choice. There was only one choice from my perspective: hold fast and rebuild what you can from the broken pieces. Stubbornness is my copilot on this journey that I did not choose for myself. A journey through hardship that will not succeed only if or when I choose to stop trying. As things are dealt to you, you feel that you have no more choices. This is one choice that I'm going to keep.

The next moments, or days, are really all a blur. The tubes come out of my face and side, this time by professional hands. It only takes a few seconds, but it feels like agonizing hours. I focus my mind on "just one more second" as I try to endure without passing out. Vomiting, which I hated so much as a child, will become a regular occurrence for me as my body adjusts to its new condition. Once that stops and the tubes are out, I'm finally able to communicate. My first words are with my

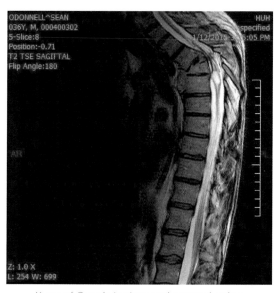

ODONNELL^SEAN
036Y, M, 000400302
5-Slice:8
Position:-0.71
T2 TSE SAGITTAL
Flip Angle:180

HUH
specified
1/12/2015   6:05 PM

AR

Z: 1.0 X
L: 254 W: 699

X-ray of Sean's broken and severed spine.

doctor. I meekly say, "What happened?" "You're lucky to be alive," he states, "You got hit riding your motorcycle 4 days ago. You are paralyzed." Ah, right to the point! The truth hits my broken pieces, and I break again. I look to my left, at my parents. Their mouths were not fixed in anger as I expected, but twisted in a combination of devastation and relief to see me alive. They had been preparing for the worst. My dad comes to me first and says, "Hang in there, son. We are going to get through this."

Now that I'm conscious, my family fills in the gaps in my memory about what happened. It was September 18th, 1995 and I was two weeks into my senior year of high school. I was generally a good kid, always trying to make my parents proud, and not overly dangerous. Sure, I had the invincibility syndrome that most 17-year-old boys have, but not to a great degree. Things *could* happen, I knew that, but probably not to me if I do things right. I had made it through some tough times growing up, so I felt street-smart and ready for what life could throw at me. I had perfect attendance and good grades in high school. Making good decisions and being smart were things I valued. I also valued living life to the fullest. Riding a motorcycle would be the ultimate embodiment of that. When I was 16 I got my license just as fast as I could. I split the cost of the motorcycle with my older brother, who was in college at the time.

It was a great sunny day – the kind of day that makes you feel glad to be alive. The kind of day that if you don't live it to its fullest potential, you will feel it was wasted. I headed out early and went the back way to school to get some windy-road time. I turned onto a street that I rode many times before. This day, there was traffic everywhere as people were settling into the grind of September, back from vacation and off to work early. As I saw people looking at me, a young kid on a motorcycle, I remember thinking, "I should gun it." In typical 17-year-old fashion, this would be a "show off" moment that I thought people would see and be impressed. I remember the last thing I thought that day: "Nah." I didn't want to increase my chances of something bad happening. That is where my memory ends on that day.

What happened next, I'm told, is someone pulled out of the traffic line without looking. As I tried to avoid the car I managed to slow to 9 mph before it T-boned me from the left. I flew off the bike into the rock filled embankment on my right. As I skidded through, relatively little damage was done to my body. I had only a few scrapes and bruises from that, namely to my left arm; however, I came to rest on a large rock that broke my back. Vertebrae T3-5 exploded in a burst fracture, damaging my aorta, lungs, and spinal cord. First time in my life I had broken anything and here I break really important things, including my spirit. From that moment, I was a complete paraplegic meaning that for the rest of my life, however short that seemed at the moment, I would never move or feel anything below my chest at the nipple level. Airlifted to a downtown hospital, my parents were told I was not expected to live but a few hours.

In that brief moment, I was taken from a relatively perfect existence that I took for granted, to a life of extreme hardship.

Now that the blank points in my memory have been filled with the truth of what I went through, I had to immediately rethink my life from long-term to short-term; big picture to small picture. My new goals were to hold fast, get through this; little steps and one at a time.

I spent 9 days in traction lying on my back while they created a brace for me to sit up. To this day, I still notice ceilings in every room. When you stare at one for that long, they become somewhat fascinating. The only entertainment I had over the long days and nights.

One particular night, a young set of nurse assistants come to my room to catheterize me, an event that happens every 4-6 hours. This particular kit empties into a bin that's placed on my stomach. The two girls are talking about their daily lives, playing little attention to me or the agony I'm feeling. As they finish, the bin of urine slips from one of their hands, spilling all over my body and face. Infected urine smells horrible and tastes even worse. They laugh as if it was an "oopsie" while again ignoring my now increased agony. They quickly pick up the trash, but leave me wet and disgusting as they quickly exit the room. When the next shift comes in to find me, they feel somewhat sorry for the condition I'm in, but more so perturbed that they have to clean me up. I'm embarrassed. I feel like a great burden to the staff because I can't do anything to help myself. I was laughed at and dejected by two assholes, and there is nothing I can do about it. I break again. I think, "How many times can I break?"

When they finally finished making the brace for my back, called a "clam-shell" (TLSO brace), I'm finally able to sit up. One small step in the direction to leave this place as fast as I can. It takes 4 people to put it on me. I sit up for the first time in 10 days. Finally, a moment that empowers me and lets me know I'm not always going to break. For the first time, I feel like there was a path to progress. I can't wait to get moving. That lasts for a few seconds before I throw up and pass out from the dizziness. My body forgot how to sit up already. When I come to, I collect myself, and try again. I last about a minute this time, before having to lie back down after another healthy vomit. Every day, one small step at a time, I struggle. Each time, I get a little further until I'm able to sit up for hours, use a wheelchair, and get as far from a hospital bed as I possibly could. I look back on my 12 days and realize through tiny steps I was able to go from near death to out of the bed. I'm starting to feel alive again. Time to leave the hospital and go to the rehab.

Rehabilitation is the time when you learn to use whatever little you have left to become independent. The days are mostly filled with boredom. You wake very early; have someone help you with urination, bowel routines, bathing, and dressing. Once you are up you get into your chair and wait for your turn with the therapist. You may have a few hours with them. The rest of the day needs to be filled. I do that with schoolwork, which was brought to me by my good friend Gerry Miller. I have full intention of getting back to school and finishing with my class that same year.

The other thing that fills my day is an endless stream of visitors. At all times, I have to receive and entertain people who only care about how I am doing and what they can do to help me in my struggle. Sometimes, I am in no condition for it. But they came to see me and offer me good energy and well wishes. I do my best to see every person. Clearly feeling love and support from your friends and family helps. However, your body is on no external schedule as it adapts to a life with a spinal cord injury. I feel an obligation to greet people who came to visit, to show them I will survive this and that I appreciate their well wishes. I did this in between fits of vomiting, bowel and bladder routines and accidents, therapy and studying. I struggle hard to hide all that not only for their sake, but for mine as well. I try to avoid embarrassment at all costs.

After visiting hours' end and the people are all gone, I have to pass time with unchosen friends that were in the same situation of recovery with you. On this night we choose to watch a movie. In an effort to do normal things, and find more comfort than a wheelchair, I try sitting on the couch in the lounge. When the movie ended, the other patients decide to play a trick on me. As a natural prankster, I enjoy a good laugh even when it involves making light of the situation I'm enduring. In order to get back into my chair, I require assistance. I ask someone if they would go tell the nurse I need help. On their way out they turn off the lights and shut the door to feign as if they would just leave me there. I laughed as I waited for the nurse to come. Minutes turn to hours. I was getting uncomfortable. I stop counting after 3 hours and start to fight the pains I'm enduring. My back is excruciating. I've not sat up this long in my TLSO brace. It digs into my armpits and back creating a sharp driving pain that feels like a rod going through my chest. It pales in comparison to the emotional pain of abandonment again. I'm breaking again, and I wasn't ready for it. I can't scream too loudly due to my condition and with the door shut, no one heard it anyway, thankfully. I can barely stand to hear my own helpless cries. Five hours or so pass when, by chance, someone comes through and finds me in that room. By now I'm soaked in urine as well. I do not go immediately to bed. I went looking for the people who left me. They were sleeping. I wake them up and simply ask "How … Why?" They say, "We forgot about you."

Of course, I break again. But this one teaches me that I now can depend on no one but myself, not even those who I would think understand my condition the most. The next day I start to teach myself how to get from any position (bed, floor, couch, or chair) back into my wheelchair. It takes a good 2 years of small steps but now in the 20 years since that day, I refuse to depend on others for basic help.

Life rarely gives you moments that convince you things are easy. Luckily, it also gives you moments that convince you that things are not impossible either. When those "impossible" moments come, they will test you and may even break you. They will also test and possibly even break those around you like friends and family to the point where you might not be able to depend on them. You have to decide how you are going to handle those possible moments. I try to be resolved to enjoy the good moments to their fullest. I'm also resolved to never give up during the hard moments either; you gain more self-reliance and depend less on help from others to keep going. It becomes your own internal drive that keeps you going.

For me, things that I learned in this journey I still take and apply every day, not only to my paralysis life, but also to my professional life. Things that we all need to develop like determination, time-management, positive attitude, critical thinking and independence are skills that you are learning right now. These are the skills that I became expert at in order to deal with my paralysis, and it is these same skills that have propelled my professional career to success. I didn't bring those traits to the table of paralysis; I learned them because of my paralysis. No valuable lesson is easy. You are learning in ways you may not appreciate at first, but if you can find the strength to embrace the lessons, you will benefit far more than what you ever lost.

The human condition is one where you have broken moments. My spine broke into the tiniest of pieces, but it reformed, healed, and is now strong enough to support me. The human spirit can also break into the tiniest of pieces, a seemingly endless amount of times, but it can also heal. Just as any bone can heal, as long as it has not turned into dust, so can any human spirit. But like a bone, it needs time and attention. It needs to be set right in order to give it the best possible recovery. As long as we are alive, we haven't turned to dust. Hold fast through your broken moments. Set your spirit's broken pieces into a way that they will reform and support you again.   This won't be easy; however, you will endure. Good luck, you can thrive and succeed!

Sean graduated from college with an engineering degree; is a successful motivational speaker and businessman; flies his own plane and runs a flight school for the physically challenged

By Thomas S. Connelly

We could not wait for our son Dan's senior year of high school. Not only did it bring all the excitement and pleasure of the upcoming college process but he had just come off an outstanding junior year on the swimming team and was designated an ALL AMERICAN! His school was recognized as having one of the top swimming programs in our whole area and Dan had already set or equaled a number of pool records, so it was with great optimism that we looked forward to even more exciting things for him that year. Dan certainly exerted the effort and he was rewarded with further improvements, but along the way we could tell physically something was not right. Athletes tend to view pain in that nothing hurts when you win so complaining is not part of their vocabulary, but again we could tell. When seeing him starting to favor his lower back when he was getting up or down, he finally did acknowledge his back was bothering him so off we went to the doctors. Sure enough they discovered that he had two small stress fractures in his lower spine so he was fitted for a removable body brace that he had to wear at all times, except naturally, when in the pool. While this took much of the pressure away from the injured area allowing some healing to begin, it itself was bulky, hot, and a burden so between the injury and the brace, not unexpectedly his event times started to drop off. It became very frustrating to him for he'd show flashes of his old self easily winning preliminary heats, then in the final events he'd finish far off the pace having run out of gas. Nonetheless, the year ended very positively with him being a valuable team captain and contributor and he had a bright future ahead of him at college.

A few weeks into his post high school summer and while taking some college courses at his new college, he accidently got hit in the groin while playing lacrosse and typically just shrugged it off. However, the pain continued and a few days later it was such that he finally took himself to the hospital and that's when the world took a turn for the worse. It was determined one of his testicles was so injured that it had to be removed immediately which was done that very evening. After a day or so of recovery, he went back to college but no sooner did he get there, we received a call from his doctor with startling news. The lacrosse stick accident may actually have been a blessing for that really was not the cause of his groin problem, testicular cancer was. The dreaded "C" word. He immediately came back home again and further tests revealed the cancer had already spread throughout his body. Every test resulted in finding more cancer and I recall in a fit of frustration asking the doctor if they tested his elbows or ear lobes yet? He said he did not understand the question which I answered almost yelling … "to just try and find somewhere that he does NOT have cancer!" One test showed that instead of his lung capacity being around 120% or more to normal as one would expect for a nationally ranked swimmer, his lung capacity was at barely 65% to normal due to all the tumors (6 large ones) which explained his recent inconsistent performance in the pool – he wasn't getting any oxygen. Here my wife and I were all proud of ourselves for insisting to look and then finding "the problem" in his back only to realize that if we/others had only looked more thoroughly, we may have discovered the much bigger problem sooner. We reluctantly had to admit that the great parental safety net turned out not to be as great as we thought. But, thank goodness for that lacrosse accident, for otherwise it may have been too late for him before the cancer was finally discovered.

We wanted healing action ASAP but what we got were tests and more tests which were needed to devise the appropriate treatment action plan and with each result it became obvious that time was not a luxury Dan had much of since he was definitely in the low percentage of survival category. His protocol called for as much chemotherapy as he could tolerate, let him recover, then start the process over again, and again. If all the chemo and other treatments worked, then surgeries would follow to cut out any and all remaining cancer areas.

We all vividly remember the day his treatments began. While nervously getting him settled into his hospital room, we were distracted by loud music coming from the room directly across the hall. After getting Dan organized, we decided to take a little walk around before the treatments started. As we left Dan's room we saw across the hall, a guy in a hospital gown sort of rocking to the music as he walked around the room … and to our surprise the music was coming from his headphones so you can imagine what his ear drums were experiencing! Anyway, he sees us, takes off the ear phones, turns down the dial, and greets us. He turned out to be a friendly and nice guy of about 25. Said he was there as a testicular cancer patient also (!) and that this was his second bout with it. He was very up and expressed total confidence in the process and the hospital, so for the first time in days we had our first taste of something positive. He then looked at Dan and point blank asked when he was going to get rid of his hair. We had not even thought of that yet so it was just one more shock to our already overloaded systems, but his next words were a most important teaching moment … *"you can let the cancer run your life, or YOU can run your life. YOU get rid of your hair. Don't let cancer do it. You be in charge of you."* Head phones back in place and music blaring, off he went back to his rocking.

Dan's first chemo cycle lasted the week and he was declining fast when we finally got him home and back in his own room, but a few hours later an entirely different person came down-stairs for dinner. It looked like Dan, but he was totally bald! The first thing he did at home was to shave all his hair off and that smile of determination gave us the hope we all needed.

For those not familiar with chemotherapy, the general idea is to give the patient as much of the deadly stuff as they can tolerate, then give them a period of time to recover and along with other healing medicines to rapidly build them back up before they knock the patient through a loop again. Any kind of chemotherapy extracts a huge toll on your systems but Dan's "cocktails" were especially brutal since they were starting way late and targeting his whole lymph gland system and most all of his "soft" organs which basically meant everything.

There are a few memorable events during his treatment that I want to share with you. Just as he was beginning his third cycle, he developed a very high fever and a further test led them to believe he may have spinal meningitis so he was immediately put into a special isolation room. There was an air lock entering his room which also had its own controlled air system. Visitors were limited and we had to be fully gowned, masked, etc. since in addition to meningitis being contagious, the chemo had also greatly reduced his immune system so being exposed to almost anything could be fatal to him since he had so little resistance. To do more accurate testing they needed to inject a large needle into his lower spine, exactly where he earlier had those stress fractures and the highway that the cancer was using to run up thru his body. Even with local anesthesia he suffered terribly through the procedure and when he was finally "out" and resting comfortably I left the hospital to get back home to our other kids while my wife stayed with Dan. I was not but a few blocks away when I got a call from her almost incoherent being so upset. I heard enough and did a dangerous and fast U-turn and ran every light back to the hospital leaving the car next to a fire hydrant. Gasping as I ran down the hall I see my wife standing outside Dan's room, arms crossed, giving off a somewhat angry vibe. She immediately tells me how upset she is at him and asks if he is allowed to do that. "Do what?" She tells me she was sitting on the far side of his room when he woke up. When she went to him he asks who it was since he couldn't tell with all the protective clothing. He tells her to at least take off the mask since it's upsetting him to no end making him feel like he's sick. She refuses saying it is necessary since he IS so sick and can't be exposed to any possible containments. He gets angry and insists that she take off her mask which she again refuses to do. He then sees and reaches over to the table for a mask and puts it on saying that if anyone has to wear a mask it will be him so she can now take off her mask. Not understanding that logic (nor approving of it!) she storms out of the room and called me. I smile and that was the moment I just knew he was going to beat this thing.

Dan started out at about 6' 1" and weighted about 160lbs, but without an ounce of fat. By about his fourth or fifth cycle he had lost a good 30 or more pounds and looked like Mr. Burns from *The Simpsons;* ashen color, no hair, even eyebrows, all hunched over with big spots all over him. It was our habit to walk as much and as often as he could tolerate. He was tethered to his interveinal tree on wheels that he also needed for stability. As we started on one walk I asked a nurse about a friend, another cancer patient we had gotten to know and learned he had recently died. "Why", I asked in surprise and was told the real question or miracle was why was Dan still alive? Attitude alone will never take the place of good medicine and care but without the right attitude, you are greatly handicapping the recovery. But with a good attitude, you are greatly improving that recovery and in some cases even changing a likely poor outcome into a positive one.

In light of all the challenges Dan was undergoing, the resulting hardships that we all were trying to cope with seem trivial in comparison. However, all of us on his "TEAM DAN" as our t-shirts proclaimed, had to successfully do each of our own parts. As the father and home provider, one of the hardest things I had to do was to find some much needed and important private time and place to drain. Attitudes are contagious so I had to be a pillar of strength and confidence in front of Dan, just as it also was essential for me to be in front of my wife, our other 4 children (3 were still at home), as well as our family and friends. They all took cues from my attitude. I did find two great places for my much needed privacy; my car to and from the hospital, and the shower. I'd exit from one or the other, force myself to stand up straight, put on a confident attitude, and face Dan, the family, the business, whatever. I would then finish with that charade and then just collapse or come unglued in my car or shower, which were my only places of refuge. I drew strength knowing Dan had it far worse.

I have the upmost respect for parents in a similar position for as the expression goes, we just have to do what we have to do. Everyone was aware of Dan's problem but if I was strong and projected confidence that he would soon be back to normal, they were not unduly worried. Now I've done a lot of hard things in my life, but a son's life-threatening problem, exacerbated by the needed leadership and outward appearance of strength and confidence that I had to project, was very, very difficult. In all honesty though, I think that most everyone in the family may have been to a degree also acting stoically in consideration for each other. My advice to all parents or spouses who may be facing a similar situation, find that needed private place of refuge to drain, then put that false façade right back on again. There is a lot more work, and acting to be done before it is over.

The next story I'd like to share happened towards the end of Dan's bout with cancer. After all the chemo and other procedures, he needed another major surgery to remove all the remaining cancer. The procedure was called an RPLD and basically they opened him from his chest to his groin, removed all intestines exposing his whole inside torso, so they could remove the whole lymph glad system which is like a mesh around the torso cavity. It is a very technical and laborious operation. Also, Dan's liver still had three remaining areas of cancer which needed to be cut, frozen, and "nuked" away depending upon those locations. In addition, multiple blood transfusions were needed while they had him opened for over 12 hours. As you can imagine, after that ordeal and after months and months of earlier medical care, Dan now looked like a shadow of his original self. Maybe just 3-4 days after the procedure when visiting with Dan, I told him I had something I needed him to start thinking about. I wanted to take a trip with him, somewhere, anywhere he wanted. Climb a mountain, shoot the rapids, run with the bulls, basically to do whatever he wanted and to go wherever. At that moment Dan had more wires and tubes in him then one could count in addition to a new about 20" gash down his stomach with all his intestines having recently been jammed back inside. He may have been down to 110 lbs. by then so it was a struggle, but he did manage to give me the "LOOK AT ME! ARE YOU FRIGGIN NUTS" look! The next day when I visited, he started by mumbling (due to the tubes in his nose and mouth) that he had decided and "we are going for the big one". Now I was at a loss since my mind was focused on him and his status that day.

"Big what"?

"THE big one, as in the biggest marlin!"

At that specific time Dan's biggest goal might have been just to be able to sit up in bed with the next milestone being to get tubes out of his nose, throat, shoulder, urinary track, and drain tubes from his stomach, then he could start working on getting unattached to the other monitors, but what was he now focused on … a big marlin! I hatched a distracting idea which turned into a goal which was way beyond just getting a stupid tube out! At that point tubes and monitors getting out and even getting better were a given, for that was not necessarily an if as much as it was a when, but a big fish though … that presented a timeless goal. And by the way, later that year we did go deep sea fishing along with my other son and in three days we caught 9 big sailfish, several mahi-mahi and yes, Dan also did catch a 300-pound marlin!

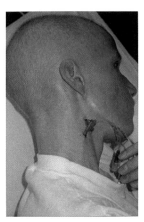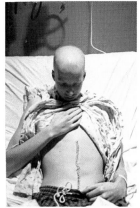

Now let me fast forward. Dan recovered, not easily, but far faster than the doctors had expected. He started physical therapy almost as soon as he got out of the hospital and probably not two months later he was also going to night school at the local university to get back in the college groove. By the time September rolled around he formally started his college career and got right back into the pool. Seems as far as he was concerned, he had some unfinished business to attend to. He not only made the Division 1 swimming team, but that freshmen year he broke his own high school time as well as equaling the college pool record.

Now I certainly don't want to minimize all the pain and difficulty Dan suffered during his bout with cancer, both physically as well as mentally, but you should also know this takes one huge toll on a family. All have to be committed to the patient's support and it comes in different ways. Just taking care of Dan was a full-time job for one or both of us. Dan's older sister was away at college but she did not miss any opportunity to either be back home or to stay in touch with her siblings checking up on their studies, schedules, and general well-being while my wife and I were so occupied caring for Dan. The younger kids somehow or other understood they needed to become more self-sufficient beyond their years and to work harder on their own to give us one less thing to worry about. Everyone in the family, from the parents down to our 12-year-old twins needed to chip in and make sacrifices, and all did this instinctively, willingly, and with smiles. All pulling together, along with Dan's already great attitude helped this ordeal be as successful as it was.

I can't say we all are better for this experience for I sure would have liked it not to have happened but that is life and as the expression goes, we learned to deal with the cards we were dealt. Dan is now happy and healthy, cancer free, married with a wonderful little son and daughter, and living a productive life. He never viewed his cancer much beyond it being just one HUGE bump in the road. He was determined to deal with it and succeed. As his first friend in the hospital advised, he was not going to let cancer either run his life nor was his fight with cancer going to define who he is today at all. As a matter of fact, very few people who have met Dan in the last few years know anything about the problem and life challenge he faced. As far as he is concerned, he saw it, and from day one he fought it, he then beat it, and he moved on.

A "STROKE" OF BAD LUCK

By Christine Crane

t was September 29th, 2006 and I was scheduled for a C-section with my second child. We knew it was going to be a girl and we already had a 2-year-old son at home. I knew it was going to be a long ride, but I didn't know just how bumpy it would turn out to be! I had a pretty normal pregnancy but she was breech so I scheduled the C-section for a week before her due date. The birth was not exceptionally difficult and we stayed in the hospital for the longest time allowed by the insurance, 5 days. We brought our precious little Audrey home on a Tuesday and were prepared for some long nights and days caring for her as well as for our little son Owen. My husband had taken the week off from work and was taking Owen to pre-school and running errands since I couldn't drive for two weeks.

We quickly started to settle into our new routine. The day after I was released from the hospital I developed an awful headache but just assumed it was the hormones and lack of sleep. However, it got worse so I called my OBGYN at 5:00 AM on Friday morning (one week almost to the minute after she was born) and told them about the headache. My OB asked if I had a fever and if my incision was infected, and I said no. His response was that it was not OB related and I should call my family doctor. I called him and he asked me to come in but I said I couldn't with the kids so he wrote me a prescription for Tylenol with codeine and made me promise if it was not better by Monday that I would come right in. The medicine controlled it enough so that the headache was just a constant mild roar instead of the blinding white hot pain that I had felt, so I could still somewhat function.

The first outing for the four of us was the Fall Festival in our town on Saturday, when Audrey was just eight days old. It was a beautiful day and the whole family had a great time. When we got home Audrey's birth announcements had arrived and my husband asked me if I wanted to see them. I looked at them but I couldn't see them very clearly since I had those "floaters" in my eyes like when you look directly into the flash of a camera. I fed the baby and went to go lie down, again thinking I was just tired. On Saturday my hormones kicked in big time and I was convinced that we were going to have an early October snowfall and little Owen did not have a winter coat. I wasn't supposed to drive for another week so I insisted that we all go to Old Navy to get him a coat before my husband was scheduled to go back to work. If you have ever been around a new mom, a word of advice: just keep quiet and go along with whatever she says! All that day I was now getting off and on pins and needles on my right side. It was like my right side was falling asleep but then it would go away, so I would just sit down and let it pass. So, there we were at Old Navy and I am pushing the cart, my husband had the baby in the stroller and my son was running around like a mad man. Rick looks over at me and says "what's wrong with your leg? You are dragging it". My response was that it had been happening on and off all day and that it would pass. He looked at me like I had lost my mind. "That's not normal, Christine. Call your mom and tell her to come right away and stay with the kids, I'm taking you to the hospital!"

We went to the community hospital, and I assumed they would think that I was just a crazy hormonal and paranoid new mom. We checked in and I told them of my symptoms and then we sat down to wait. When they called to take my vitals they took my pulse first and the nurse asked if my heart was racing. "No," I replied. She then took my blood pressure and the nurse got this weird look on her face. She called another nurse over and they took it again, then they both looked at each other in panic! Well, everything moved pretty quickly after that. They stuck a nitroglycerine pill under my tongue, put me on a gurney, and rushed me back. Apparently my blood pressure was off the charts, so much so that I was not even supposed to be conscious with those numbers. Lots of doctors came in and out. Shortly CAT scans, MRI's, blood tests, and reflex tests were done along with lots of questions, but they had no idea what was going on. They admitted me but through the night things got worse. I had parts of my right side shaking (called posturing), weakness, slurring and numbness. The thing that they couldn't figure out was that one minute I seemed perfectly fine and the next I couldn't speak, but the scans showed nothing!

After another day there they transferred me to the local large teaching hospital and now I'm really starting to panic. We got there, more tests and questions and the shooting pain was still getting worse and more frequent but still no answers. It was now Tuesday and that night the headache got so bad that they had to tie me down to the bed and give me sedatives. After that my memory is spotty, until about mid-October. From what my family and friends were told, my prognosis was not good and "if" I even lived, the chances were high that I would have major brain damage; would not be able to communicate; and probably need to be in a continuous-care facility for the rest of my life, however long that would be. It turned out that I had a very rare condition called a postpartum cerebral angiopathy which caused a vasospastic stroke. In layman's terms, the blood vessels in my brain would constrict and then reopen. It took the doctors a while to figure this out because in the beginning it seemed that every time I was in a scan the vessels happened to be open, until they weren't! They treated me with a powerful cocktail of steroids to profuse my brain with blood and to keep the vessels open to try to prevent brain death. I woke up about a week later with the mother of all headaches, attached to all kinds of monitors and drip-lines. I didn't have the ability to move or speak; didn't have any idea where I was or what was happening. It was just a terrifying experience being at least semi "there" but without anyone realizing it. I did know just enough though, to know this was not good at all.

It turned out that I had a number of strokes of varying sizes on both sides of my brain, the largest being in the left hemisphere which left a tangerine size section of dead brain cells in the middle area. Over the next six weeks I was in the ICU continuing to get pumped with steroids and other medications through a port in my neck.

One of the things that is different about a TBI (Traumatic Brain Injury) which is what I had, from say a spinal cord injury or a catastrophic illness is that in this condition, some people around you including even some of the nurses and doctors think you do not understand what they are saying because you appear "out". However, we often can understand, so to all those around us, thank you for your help but please don't act like we are not in the room, it is very demeaning. Even if we cannot communicate, the chances are we at least to some degree can understand what is going on around us and it is very scary!

Every stroke is different but the thing every stoke survivor has in common is, as with many dramatic events, the original "you" is gone. Hopefully the core of what makes you "you" is still intact and is still there some place, but it is just trapped.

By the time they finally decided that medically I was able to leave the hospital and go to rehabilitation, I had minimal motor and communication skills, and I could do absolutely nothing about taking care of myself. So here I am, a new mother with a little boy at home along with my newborn baby that I hardly even had enough time to bond with, and the one who should have and so desperately wanted to take care of them, is now needing full care herself and is being shuffled from one medical facility to another like a parcel.

I was totally distraught and terrified by the time I got to rehab! There was a comfort level and degree of security back in an ICU, for I always had company since there was always someone coming to give me meds or check my vitals. When I got to the rehabilitation hospital though, the impact and realization of my lost independence finally and totally hit me. When you are in the hospital you know that it is temporary and when you are well enough that they will release you. It struck me then that this, the way I was then, might be as good as I was ever going to get. I needed help with everything, I couldn't even go to the bathroom, dress or even stand without help. How was I going to take care of my kids! That was the first time I remember crying, not because of pain or frustration, but the whole concept of me and my care being totally dependent on others; even just being where I was instead of being at home where I should be. I had others that needed ME, not the other way around.

My first week in rehab was also Thanksgiving, so it was pretty desolate since they only had a skeleton staff. I couldn't sleep thinking of my husband, little Owen, and my new baby Audrey, and that was when I decided that I had to take control of my future. They needed me and I needed them. I could wallow in the fact that this terrible thing had happened to me and that it was so unfair, or, I could get to work! Many people have asked, how did you stay so positive and never do the "why me" thing? Well, that is a question all of us ask ourselves, but there is no answer to be found. The solution though is to actually do something about it. So right then I made up my mind and got to work.

I got up, worked hard, and eventually learned how to take care of myself. With a positive attitude I went to therapy every day even though some days I was so exhausted I was ready to cry. My limbs would shake and I had such a headache just from trying to concentrate on what people were saying. I even asked for extra therapy on the weekends. I relearned how to put on makeup and did so most every day (with my left hand no less) even though I rarely wore it before unless we were going out. Self-pride, not self-pity. On the days I didn't have therapy I would go to the library and get out kids' books and try to iden- tify the letters and numbers. I had to learn how to read and write all over again but this time using my non dominate hand. One of the hardest things I had to learn was sequencing; the order in which things are done, like brushing your teeth. For most people it just comes automatically because you have been doing it for so long. You don't even have to think about it, like when you drive to a place you go to so often you hardly even remember getting there, but when your brain has been wiped clean, nothing comes automatically. It is like teaching a child. I often say that my kids and I learn many things together. I think that one of my big motivators is to be a good role model to them. To show them that no matter what life throws at you, you need to put on your big boy pants, try your absolute best, and work as hard as you can to defy expectations. You just have to find that strength in yourself because no one else can do it for you. I did have a great support system with all my family and friends, especially my husband and my mom, but they can't do it for you and the only way I was going to get back to my role of wife and mom was to earn it myself. The doctors and therapists can give you the tools to get there but they can't make you get out of bed and do it. And saying "it just takes hard work", believe me is one huge understatement. No, it takes a hell of a lot more than that! It also takes patience, self-love and respect, people you can lean on and the determination to get up and keep going even if you fall again, and again! I have always been a pragmatic person, so in my lowest times I thought "Ok, if I give up, what would that look like"? I did not find the answer acceptable, and still don't, so I keep pushing.

I was always also a very independent person; I don't like to ask for help. This situation though taught me that it is OK to ask for help, everyone needs help sometimes and there is no shame in asking for it. It also taught me patience; everything is slower with one hand. I also learned to be more open minded and not to judge people so harshly, you don't know their story. I am not glad at all that I had the strokes but I do like who I am today and I think I am a better person because of it.

When this journey began I was not supposed to live through the night; then that I was going to have to be in a continuous-care facility; then, that I was not going to be able to be left alone or even take care of my own children. Two years after my journey began I got my driver's license back and got rid of the nanny that was helping every day with my children. I am now walking without a brace and go to the gym a few times a week. I still see improvements everyday even now almost 10 years later. The key I think is to find the thing that makes you want to fight. That something is different for everyone but I think we all have it in us, it just hasn't been called upon in all of us yet. So, I implore you to find your something and get to work. It is so worth it!

Good luck!

"LIFE WAS GOOD"

By Edward DiDonato

ife was good. I had just graduated from college. I ended my college career on a high note as I was the captain of my university's lacrosse team; we had won our conference; went to the NCAA tournament, and I received all-conference recognition. I then got to enjoy a summer of coaching lacrosse and beginning the search for my first "real" job which I shortly found. Yes, life was good. Unfortunately though, things would change in the blink of an eye.

In early January of the next year, there was a big college basketball game of my former university, which I was now a proud alumnus. The game was on a Sunday and the day before an old teammate came into town with a friend for a little reunion. I was living in the suburbs of Philadelphia with a couple guys, and with one of my roommates we all decided to go out in Philly for the evening. We had a blast catching up, talking about old times, and just enjoying the company of friends old and new. The night flew by, and before we knew it was time to head home. Upon leaving we tried to hail a taxi but while waiting, one of my buddies decided to entertain us by doing some pull-ups on some construction scaffolding that was over the sidewalk, which gave us all a good laugh. A young lady, we did not know came up and decided to join him doing pull-ups, which made us laugh even more. Our laughter was quickly inter-rupted though by the yelling of a guy from her group demand-ing the girl stop and get down, which she quickly did, but his rant continued at both her and us. We were all taken aback by his yelling at her and then at us. He focused his anger towards my college teammate who was doing pull-ups, but my current roommate immediately stuck up for him. Now my roommate and this random guy were in a bit of a screaming match, which was really dumb considering how it started, but there we were. The exchange of words lasted no more than a minute, but as we started to leave I heard a friend of this random guy telling him to "put it away." I looked back and saw he had a gun drawn on my roommate. With my hands open and up, I said something along the lines of, "what are you going to do with that, shoot someone?" In hindsight it was a dumb question, for he answered my question by pointing it at me and firing twice in quick succession. The first shot hit my right hand then my right shoulder with the second shot. I started falling forward and then in quick succession he fired four more bullets into my abdomen as I was going down. My first instincts were to get back up but the lower half of my body was not responding. One of my friends kept telling me to not move. My memory at that time was not as much about the pain but instead looking in amazement at my own blood gushing out onto the sideway from my shirt and jeans. There was an intense burning sen-sation but I guess adrenaline kept me from feeling real pain. Instead, the fears of what may further happen engulfed me. As I laid there on the pavement I pleaded with my friends, "Don't let me die here." As I watched the blood leave my body I knew this was bad. How bad? I had no idea but my focus at that time was to simply not die. Fortunately the police were on patrol in the area and they were there in just a few minutes. The EMT was called and they too arrived very quickly which literally saved my life. One of my friends told them he was my brother which allowed him to travel in the ambulance with me and I recall him constantly asking me things like my address to try and keep me awake. One minute I was casually walking on the street enjoying the company of friends; the next minute I'm shot six times, gushing blood, struggling to stand, and being whisked away in an ambulance in critical condition; the whole episode of which could not have been 15 minutes. My "Life was good" had taken a major life altering change.

Upon arrival at the hospital I was immediately sedated and prepped for surgery. Afterwards I was also placed into a med-ically-induced coma and kept that way on and off for over twenty days. I remember little from those days but was told when I would occasionally come to, that I was totally confused. What happened? Where was I? I had tubes coming out of every-where. I couldn't even speak with the tubes in my mouth and nose. I had even been strapped down a couple times as I tried to move in my medicated state. When I was finally eased out of the coma, I found out that I already had nine major surgeries. Half of my right lung had been removed. Most of my liver was removed and they resected a good portion of my small intes-tines. I was further shocked that the surgeons needed to split my abdomen in half, placing the two sections on either side and over my rib cage to gain full entry to all of the rest of my internal organs and damaged areas, and pretty much kept it open since they had to revisit all the damaged areas so often.

I don't recall just when, but the internal bleeding finally stopped but everything was still so swollen and traumatized they could not fully close my stomach. They actually didn't finally close the wound until nine months later. In the meantime, I lived with what I called my "pregnancy belly". Eventually skin from my leg would be slowly and carefully grafted over my open stomach wound but without much of any stomach muscles available to hold everything in, I can't describe just how awful it looked. You could see my intestines moving through the thin skin, and I was horrified with my appearance. I looked like a human Frankenstein. My appearance was the least of my problems though. Since many of my organs had been removed, resected, and/or relocated I had tubes coming out of everywhere. I had no ability to eat; digest food; have any control whatsoever of body waste; much movement from my waist down; or even being able to just sit up due to my open and "pregnant belly". As frightening as all that was, it did not compare to the realization that one leg was not moving well, which by the way, was my good leg. The other leg; I was not able to move at all, as in nothing. One of the bullets (which is still in me) came to rest in my lower spine and it did considerable damage to my spinal nerves.

After three months and four more surgeries, I was deemed "well enough" to be moved to the Spinal Cord Injury floor at their rehabilitation hospital. The primary focus of my medical team at Jefferson was to save my life so rehabilitating my legs was not as big a priority.. I just assumed that once my stomach was back together I'd get up and they would be just fine. I had no idea what a journey I would embark on. Now I'll forever be grateful to all the outstanding medical professionals for saving my life and their excellent care, but it was time to start on the very long and hard road back. I was nervous and concerned as I had grown comfortable at the hospital, but I needed to make this next step.

Physically I was a total mess, but over the next many months I'd learn more about myself mentally, and emotionally than I knew existed. A big part of recovery is time and therapy, but the range and degree of recovery success greatly varies from patient to patient. Now, with each injury there are reasonable expectations we should have for our recoveries, but we should seize every opportunity to maximize our ability to recover each and every day. How I dealt with and achieved success within that range that is what I'd now like to share.

I was dealt a very bad hand but what was I now going to do with it? I'll assume that the only persons reading this book have themselves been dealt some kind of a bad hand so there's not much need to go further into my own injuries and medical problems since you probably already understand those challenges. The how and the degree of a bounce back though is important. Yes it was hard, sometimes very hard physically, emotionally, and mentally. There were many times I hurt terribly, and there were many tears, and there were also many why me moments of despair and depression. The staff at my rehab clinic were excellent getting me through much of that, but here are some other elements that really helped my bounce back and hopefully will also help you.

> *Therapy will be long, hard, and very painful but the professionals are excellent and know just when, how, and how much to push you. Trust them. Listen to them. Then push yourself harder*

> *There will be plenty of days you just don't want to move let alone go through more therapy. Don't give up. Go to the therapy even if you don't perform at your highest level. A bad therapy session is always better than NO therapy session. Your room can quickly become your safe house and you get very comfortable there. It is easy to feel that most anything outside that safe house represents difficulty, pain, frustration, and embarrassment. It actually is just the opposite. Get comfortable being uncomfortable. Waiting for you outside of your safety zone is the only place you'll find independence, freedom, and self-sufficiency to the most degree that you can achieve. Don't settle for anything less. Get up and go do it!*

> *Consistency is VERY important. I've never naturally been the smartest, fastest, strongest, or really the best at anything. The reason for my success is that I show up and work hard EVERY DAY. It earned me the*

nickname of "Everyday Ed," from a buddy on my college lacrosse team and I see it being even more true in who I am today. If you don't show up, you fall behind, and you will not restart your therapy right where you left off but instead you will be further back. Recovery is hard work, but regression is very easy if you do not continue your hard work. Days will be hard, days will be bad, but keep at it. The accumulation of the work is the end goal. Nothing is achieved in one day, rather it is that accumulation of days that build something great! I've seen people with many of the same injuries as mine and much of the difference within their success range can be attributed to mental fortitude, determination, and a positive attitude, which is all up to you. Take CONTROL!

➢ *Any limitations I was given only pushed me that much harder. Some I surpassed and others I did not, but that was most definitely not because I didn't work hard every day. I have a clear head because when I look back there is not much more that I could have done. Regardless of the pain I knew that these therapies and the great people helping me was the way I was going to improve and if I didn't take advantage of that then I was only keeping myself from reaching my full potential.*

After a little more than 100 days in the hospital and seven more weeks at rehab, I was making progress on walking. I had learned how to take care of my own personal hygiene, which may not seem like a big deal but it truly was one huge milestone in my path to self-sufficiency and dignity. I could dress myself for the most part. All of these small things gave me back my independence, little by little. I was getting stronger and between the therapy, braces, crutches or cane, I was able to stand and move about. It may not have been pretty but it made all that hard work, worthwhile. There was progress, and I could see it. Then one day I was presented with another huge and scary challenge; they were taking me out in public. We went outside the safety and confines of the clinic to get reac-quainted with the world with my new physical ailments. They took me to a park and then to a building with an escalator, all of which was terrifying. The world seemed to be moving a million miles an hour. I was very self-conscious of how I looked, fearful of strangers, and unsure how I could possibly live in the outside world on a day-to-day basis. Hopefully you will not experience that fright, but if so, it only highlights how comfortable (and a barrier to your recovery) that your safe place can become. Leave it, and get out there.

Family and Friends: I was fortunate having a very strong family and friends support group but this can also be a two-edged sword for they are not professionals and therefore may not understand all the issues you are going thru. It can sometimes get very frustrating but try to handle them as calmly as you can. There can be and probably will be some arguments but they care and mean well. Emotions are high, and they struggle right along with you. They offer far more positive benefits than not having them around. So, if you're lucky to have people around, keep it light and enjoy the company. Positivity is the name of the game in your recovery so take the support and help but leave any insensitive remarks or misunderstandings of what you are going through at the door.

Another thing I found that you may also experience, maybe more so with the friends, is that some may never have truly been there for you in the first place. I lost many "so-called friends" after my incident and during my recovery. My situation made people uncomfortable and I was no longer the same man I once was. The Eddie that was always ready to be part of the party was dead and gone. Yes, I had changed for I now had more important goals, to regain my health and live a life worth living. This is not to put down theirs or even my own earlier lifestyle but it no longer became a focus, and it would only hurt me and my continuing recovery. I wanted to walk again, I wanted to work out again, and I wanted to see the things that this beautiful earth has to offer. Now, as I realized many people

I considered friends were in reality just party buddies and it did hurt. Take that commonality away and there was little left. I perceived betrayal and there was pain, but the focus should be on the ones who do care and stick by your side. Focus on the support and strength of the loved ones who show care by their actions because if you allow yourself to get wrapped up in those that don't care about you then you will become bitter and maybe even enough to prevent you from accomplishing what YOU truly need.

Mentors: I didn't have any mentors in my progress other than seeing, meeting, and learning from other patients. We all were from different backgrounds and with different injury levels, but we had common ground in our struggle trying to regain some normalcy in our lives. People with more devastating injuries than myself, reminded me to be thankful for the ability to even have some limbs to move and this really put my injuries in perspective. I shifted from lamenting about what I didn't have to being thankful for what I did have. There were people who were there for a second, third, fourth time and I saw their struggle. Naturally I gravitated to those with positive attitudes, as they seemed to be making the most progress. There were still many that refused to put in the work, and in their frustrations gave the nurses and therapists a tough time. They did not seem to be as successful. In some ways it's understandable as you are very vulnerable and it is a very trying time, but in the end where does having a bad attitude get you? In my opinion it got those people nowhere. All of these people, both the ones with positive attitudes as well as those maybe not, helped me as I could put my injuries in perspective, and see that, remaining positive, and working hard was the only way I might get better. Obviously, there are no guarantees, but I never want to look back and say to myself I wish I had worked harder at this or put more effort in because those "what-if's" will last a lifetime. *"Attitudes are contagious; is yours worth catching?"* Seek out those with the positive attitudes and then do your best to spread that attitude to others.

Goals: Most definitely set goals as soon as you can. They must be as high but also as realistic and achievable as is possible. Early on in your recovery it could be something as simple as wiggling your toe, or maybe just being able to sit up but take pride in each accomplishment, then set newer goals. Little successful steps will lead to bigger triumphs. I had set small, medium, hard, and then really hard goals and as I'd progress I'd recalibrate the goal plan. I did not achieve all but did reach most of even my really hard ones. One I'm most proud of came to me after seeing a story and pictures of another guy who had also been shot several times in the stomach and had similar torso problems as me, but now was a bodybuilder. There was also a marathoner who was hit on his bike, but now he had a "six pack" for a stomach and had just run another marathon. Well, given my mobility issues, a marathon is not in my future but I was determined to prove the doctors wrong. It took me a few years but I've got that "six pack," and have even competed in a regional bodybuilding contest! Goals! Set them realistic but high, then do it. Now I'll never say I'm happy with the things that happened to me. I will say though, that overall I'm better for the experience. I don't recommend anyone run out and getting shot 6 times for I sure wish that was not me but I have to say despite losing a few years and having the legacy of all the digestive, health, and mobility problems that I have, that I think I am a better person today than I was before. Life is anything but the same but nonetheless … ***Life is Great!***

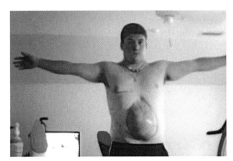

"TOO YOUNG FOR THIS"

By Kate Knetzger

was flattered and humbled to be invited to share my story for this book. It is an honor to have my story included next to those of these remarkable individuals. Each story is different but carries with it the theme of medical adversity. In many ways we have all fought and conquered a similar fight, for it is not the health problem we are sharing but instead it is how we have exceeded what was expected of us. My story is a little different, for my health problems lie not only in my rear view mirror, but are current, and have promised to return. There is no question "if" I will continue to face health problems, but rather "when" and "how often." Today, at the age of twenty-eight, I have had five major surgeries, three of which are joint replacements. The arthritis that has robbed me of my childhood "normalcy" is a monster whose damage I will continue to face for the rest of my life. My story is not as much about reaction to a problem in the past but instead, facing it coming at me.

I vividly remember the day when I realized I wasn't like everyone else. That my legs didn't work as well as they were supposed to. I was thirteen years old, and had just begun my freshman year of high school. We were in an outside class studying plants and my classmates all squatted down on their knees to get a better look. I looked at them perplexed, wondering how their bodies moved like that. How did their knees bend in that way? Wasn't it painful? As I went to imitate their movement, pain and limitation stopped me before I could even get halfway down. My joints felt stiff and restricted. That day, the thought came and went, and I was blissfully unaware that this was a sign of something much bigger.

The coming months magnified my physical insufficiencies. I wanted desperately to participate in all the activities and sports like my friends but the more I tried, the more my hips and knees would ache relentlessly. By age fourteen, running was out of the question, and so the sports that I had loved and enjoyed were no longer an option. Determined to be a part of a team, I tried out for and made the cheerleading team. By senior year, I was the proud captain of the varsity cheerleading team, but found myself on the sidelines more and more, as the joint pain debilitated me.

I finally saw an orthopedic surgeon who was surprised to see that the range of motion in my legs was about half of what is considered "normal" for someone my age. X-Rays revealed severe joint space narrowing in my hips and knees similar to that of someone in their seventies and eighties who had undergone the wear and tear of everyday life, also known as osteoarthritis. More tests followed and it was finally determined I had Juvenile Idiopathic Arthritis, which basically meant "arthritis in someone who is young for which the cause unknown." In an attempt to find relief from my daily pain, I was prescribed a high dosage of a potent drug used mostly for cancer patients.

Unfortunately, the drugs brought on a myriad of side effects, which added to my physical suffering, and provided little relief of my joint pain. As my physical health deteriorated, I was plagued by frustration and self-doubt. I desperately tried to fit in with my peers and the day-to-day activities that I once took for granted.

At the ripe old age of fourteen, I was a candidate for double hip replacement surgery. John Hopkins Hospital was considered the top location for my kind of problem but until I had finished growing, all they could do for me was to attempt to shave off "extra bone" in my hip with the hope that the procedure would improve my range of motion and therefore alleviate some pain. My surgeon at the time, whom I greatly respected, humbly admitted that this was a learning experience for him and his team, for they had never seen a clinical picture quite like mine. There were no guarantees this procedure would work but looking forward to the potential of feeling better, I left his office that day with a surgery date and for the first time in months, a glimmer of hope.

I had the surgery that June, and spent the whole summer recovering from the surgical procedure while trying to regain my strength and flexibility. By about week eight, my range of motion improved marginally and so did the pain but tests showed the improvement was not significant. It was immediately clear to me that this was just the tip of my medical iceberg, something I could not fully comprehend at the time. Despite the lack of significant gain from the surgery, I took away from that time one of the first glimpses into my personal strength and courage. I'll never forget what my surgeon said as I left my last post-operative visit, "The team and I wanted to tell you that we don't think this could have been done without your positivity and determination." He explained that my optimistic outlook and strong will to get better gave him confidence in me as a patient, and motivated him to do a surgery unlike any he had done before. Motivation and optimism opens doors.

In the years that followed, my optimism continued, but my joints got worse, and so did my restrictions in cheerleading and even simple activities of daily living. I was in and out of doctors' offices, and icepacks were my constant companion, but I did my best to not let this stop me from having as normal of a high school experience as possible. By junior year I began to explore my interest in becoming a nurse, and applied to nursing schools. Several doctors advised me that this career would not be compatible with my health restrictions, but with all do respect, I listened to my heart, and sought after my new goal.

By the time I started college nursing school, I was on a very specialized regimen of weekly shots and trial medicines. While my peers would nap or study in between classes, I would make a trip to the infirmary, where I knew all the doctors and nurses on a first name basis. While the medications helped my joint pain, they were immunosuppressive, and brought on regular bouts of bronchitis and other respiratory infections. Without quick and careful attention to balancing my health and medications, I'd get pneumonia. As nice as the staff were, I can vouch that being confined to a college infirmary is not the best way to enjoy college life! As a college freshman three hours from home, I quickly learned to be my own advocate and the importance of autonomy. My new friends and the positive college support system helped offset the many hospital visits and constant difficulty and pain of getting around but nonetheless, time did fly by.

After senior year, while my friends went on to enjoy their summers before they started in "the real world", I had different plans. My graduation gift was not a watch, a scrapbook, or another memento of my fun filled years. No, my graduation "gift" was going to be the recipient of a new pair of hips!

On August 5th of 2009, with as much fortitude and determination as I could muster, I slowly hobbled into the Hospital for Special Surgery (HSS) in NYC to have a double hip replacement surgery. Several of the pre-operative staff offered me a wheelchair to get from room to room, but I graciously declined. I woke up later that night, packed in bandages and attached to tubes, groggy from the anesthesia. To my utter shock and surprise, one of my first visitors the next morning was a physical therapist who exclaimed that she was there to get me out of bed to walk! While the thought of walking with new hips was daunting at first, I was quickly reassured and overcome with gratitude – it was only one day after surgery, and I was walking with less pain than I had had in years. If I felt this good one day after surgery, I knew that there were many days without pain in my future.

Rehabilitation was a test not only physically, but emotionally as well. I was on a hip and knee replacement rehab unit, and was approximately forty years younger than the next youngest person there. This brought scrutiny from the other patients in my unit, who could not comprehend that someone so young could have undergone the same surgery as them. On the wheelchair ride to "group rehab" each morning, I would prepare myself to explain to them something that I still did not fully understand myself.

My quality of life quickly improved, and within six weeks I was functioning better than I had in years! With renewed energy and determination I dove into my Registered Nurse Certification studies and successfully passed the test that enabled me to carry out my dream of being a nurse. I was excited to start my career, and hoped that my perspective as a patient would help me to better understand what my own patients were going through.

Seven weeks after my hip replacements, my newfound strength and hopefulness were shattered in a single moment. I was out with friends, and had recently been freed of my "post-op restrictions" by my orthopedic surgeon. One moment I was talking with friends out at a restaurant, and the next, I had slipped on a puddle of water causing me to land on my right side. While this was not a traumatic fall, the way I landed caused my new hip prosthetic to go through my right femur, shattering it into pieces. Thirty minutes later, an ambulance wheeled me into the nearest emergency room where the on-call surgeon hovered over me under bright lights. "You will need a surgery, and this surgery will definitely be a harder recovery than your two total hip replacements." The words cut through me like knives. All of my hard work was decimated by an accidental fall. Through the fog of the pain medications, I replayed the fall in my head over and over again, and questioned what I could have done to avoid it. What if I hadn't gone out with my friends that night? What if I went to my sister's instead? After some hours of self-torture, I gave myself a reality check. The reality was, I *couldn't* change the situation. So what was the use in being consumed by self-pity and blame? The truth is, in order to become our best selves; we must *accept* ourselves for who we are, and where we are in relation to where we want to be.

When I finally got in this mindset, my attitude changed from "why me" to "let's do this." I was transferred to HSS the next day, and scheduled for surgery as an "add-on" for that night.

The surgeon from the emergency room was indeed right, the recovery from my broken femur was longer, more arduous, and more painful than I ever could have expected. I worked tirelessly to gain strength in my leg, while applying for nursing jobs. My first choice was to work at HSS, where I had been a patient twice in the last two months. The kindness, professionalism, and skill of the nurses played a large role in my immediate post-operative period. I knew that as a nurse at HSS I could combine my skill set and personal experiences to give back to others who were having orthopedic surgeries. What could be better than that?

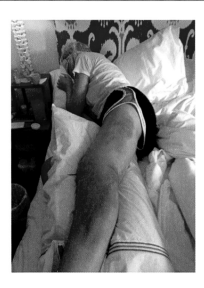

Towards the end of my recovery from my broken leg, I was offered a job as an RN on the very floor where I was a patient. I did not often speak of my personal experiences to my patients, but in the rare occasion I did, I was grateful for the encouragement and hope that it would instill in the patients who were struggling like I was just a few months earlier. Each day, I felt lucky to be doing something I loved while giving back to others.

A year passed, and my hips and legs continued to feel great. I loved being a nurse, and I loved working at HSS. I was surrounded by patients whose lives, like mine, were transformed by elective surgeries, and felt grateful to be a small part of that transformation. But to my great dismay, I began to feel pain again. This time, the pain was in my left knee. I knew there was some arthritis there but it was hoped that once the hip problems were fixed, it would relieve the pressure and stress on my knees. While that was true initially, it was clear that my knee was decompensating quickly. I could not bear the thought of another surgery and so soon after I had gotten into a normal state of life. So, I hid my swollen knee under a tightly wrapped ace bandage, and smiled through twelve-hour shifts, never wanting my patients to see me in pain. Clearly, I was in denial and preventing my own needs to be met.

I finally succumbed and went back to my surgeon who informed me I needed a total knee replacement. The arthritis in my left knee was severe in all three compartments, and he was surprised that I had worked as long as I did. The thought of another big surgery was devastating and daunting, especially because I knew that this recovery would be longer and harder than the double hip replacements. After that visit with my doctor, I cried daily, and informed my boss at HSS that I would be taking leave from work. Because I could not work, I had to move out of my apartment and away from my friends. Upon arriving home, I promptly went into a state of depression. The trap of self-pity that had consumed me with my broken leg had taken over without me even realizing it. It was two weeks after arriving home that it hit me like a ton of bricks. I was going to a store downtown with my mom, and she parked two blocks away. My heart sank as I anticipated the pain that would come with walking these two blocks. Wait a second! I was twenty-three years old, and just a year prior I was walking over a mile without difficulty! Something had to change, and I was the only one who needed to make that decision. That day, I *accepted* where I was, and where I needed to be. Within the week, my total knee replacement was booked, and the only place I was looking to, was ahead and to a life of better health.

Well, here I am today, and as I said at the very beginning. This is really where my contribution to this book really begins. While I have already had to deal with a number of medical and health issues, it is what lies ahead of me and how I plan to deal with them and why, is what I'd like to share. Based on my medical condition and even if it is to some degree stabilized, there is no question that I will face surgeries and recoveries for the rest of my life. I am expecting to be on an almost regular surgical routine, as in a few years of strength and stability, followed by another joint replacement surgery with subsequent pain, therapy, and recovery. I then hope to have another few years of quality life before I'm back with another year of pain and lost time. I have been told by friends, family and Doctors that I am courageous in how I have handled my medical adversity, but I disagree. I am simply doing what I have to do in order to make my good years count.

I have a loving heart, joy, and zest for life, and I refuse to let my degenerative disease take that away. I am in control – not the disease. By my thirtieth birthday, I will have likely had four joint replacements; all with limited "shelf-lives" and the knowledge that they will all need revisions at some point in time. That said, by my thirtieth birthday, I will also have loved deeply, traveled, fostered friendships, and pursued my career with fervor and humility. I would be lying if I said I was not afraid of the pain that has promised to return, but I refuse to let this overtake me. I encourage anyone who is facing medical adversity to always *look forward* to the possibility of better health. In the coming years, I will not waste time with self-pity, but will accept things for how they are, with the knowledge that this will serve me in getting to where I want to be. I have, and will make the good times count.

SOME CONCLUDING COMMENTS AND OBSERVATIONS

By Gregory D. Snyder, MD

In this collaboration, we have sought to draw upon the insights of our injuries and illnesses to offer you a better understanding of what perils and promise lay ahead. Our common bond is that we have experienced unexpected and unwelcome change in our lives and personal circumstances due to devastating disease and injury, but have used these experiences to add strength to our lives and personal relationships by focusing on what is most important in life, as we recover. Recently, I recounted these and similar stories, including my own, to a friend who had not experienced similar hardship; her reflection on these stories is true – "when given a lemon, some people can make lemonade, but these stories are about people making margaritas!"

I suffered a spinal cord injury at 27 years of age when I fell down an abandoned quarry while hiking with my dog. I don't remember the exact circumstances surrounding my injury (an apparently common phenomenon for many people with traumatic events), but I do think that I was likely climbing without proper safety equipment. I broke my back at the T12 vertebra and was taken urgently to the teaching hospital where I was a medical student at the time; this dramatic change in my life due to unforeseen spinal cord injury came at the end of my third year of medical school. I was revived at my medical school's hospital, underwent several surgeries, and was discharged to a rehabilitation hospital for several weeks before beginning a year of outpatient therapy. Afterwards, I returned to medical school in a wheelchair with complete paralysis below my waist, finished my 4th year of med school, and started Internal Medicine residency to continue my training as a doctor.

Sustaining this injury and becoming a patient myself at the same time I was training to be a doctor offered me unique insights into the patient experience from the patient's perspective, as well as that of the providers who seek to help patients during experiences like those stories included in this booklet. In truth, we are *all* patients – all of us – in different ways, at different times, and whether we know it or not. On the other hand, the providers at your rehabilitation hospital are powerless to help effect positive recovery and rehabilitation for you without your added will. The personal strength of patients, oftentimes empowered by family and friends, usually determines the level and degree of patient success stories. As we have learned in this booklet, the ability of each contributor to push forward, accept the vulnerability of trying new things or difficult rehabilitative tasks, and meet the emotional perils of recovery head-on is what allowed them to move forward to redefine themselves, positively. This is not easy to do, but that is why it is necessary.

My story of spinal cord injury is similar to the stories of Eddie, Christine, Sean, Kate, and Tom's, in that we all experienced with ourselves or a loved one, a crash course with the healthcare system, tried to learn a new vocabulary of medical words that were unfamiliar to us (even as a student of medicine), entertained visitors in the hospital when we didn't feel like doing so for one reason or another, and tried to strike a balance between distracting ourselves from our unfortunate change in circumstance with using that change as a source of strength and motivation to continue our recovery. We all experienced a paralyzing moment when reality set in and we realized the truth of our health dilemma. We all feigned stoicism, or pretended to be strong when we truly felt weak. We all sought strength from loved ones – family and friends – but also experienced the loss of friends who lacked empathy as well as the difficulty of addressing family who didn't quite understand things from our perspective. We have all been exhausted with re-learning tasks that others find simple or take for granted. We have though, all gained insight and strength from these experiences.

Rehabilitation and recovery is an ongoing process that begins with your injury or illness, but does not end when you leave the rehabilitation hospital. In some ways, we are fortunate to experience rehabilitation, because it improves our understanding of our new bodies, makes us more attuned to our health and overall wellbeing, and, in many cases, brings us closer to the family and friends that matter. We meet other patients who have been through similar situations, and learn things from people whom we would have never met. Most of us never thought we would be in the situations we are now in, none of us wanted this set of circumstances to unfold, but all of us are stronger for having faced them.

A few final parting words of collective advice from us, as you continue on your path of recovery.

Purpose

- **It is essential you set a realistic goal and then work to exceed it, with determination**

- **As quickly as possible, get past the "why me" and the what you don't have; focus on the new me and the good you can experience and share**

Therapy

- Set daily and weekly goals; re-calibrate your standards if need be

- Keep moving forward by trying different things with your therapists

- Try to *understand* your injury or illness medically; inform yourself

Mental Health

- Meet with mental health experts; they can help you with your "bounce"

- If you don't feel comfortable with a therapist, talk to friends/family

- Seek out mentors with similar backgrounds to guide you in recovery

Support

- It is OK and normal to have bad days, just make sure these don't become every day

- If you have family that want to help you, you are lucky; accept their support

- If that positive support is not readily available, that is all the more reason to work for your self-sufficiency and pride.

- If your friends don't understand, that's OK, because it's difficult to know what you're going through without you telling them; be patient with them

Family and Friends

- Your help and care is most appreciated and important but please also bring a good working knowledge not only of our medical conditions but also our mental and emotional needs

- Sometimes a helping hand is appropriate, other times it might be a push, and at others it might be just respecting our privacy. Know the best timing for each

General Comments

- You *will* exit your "safe house" if you're working hard; accept vulnerability

- Recovery of your strength includes your mind, body and spirit

- "The key is to find things that make you want to fight..."

- Support from others is helpful; strength from within is essential

- Don't settle for just lemonade! Aim and work higher!

ACKNOWLEDGEMENTS

It is with a great sense of appreciation that we would like to acknowledge and thank the medical staff and our friends at the below listed medical facilities. Without their superb care we may not even be here let alone being able to share with you some of the extra reasons for our return to good health. We send a collective thank you to all at these outstanding healthcare institutions that we encountered along our journey back to good health.

Thomas Jefferson University Hospital, Philadelphia, PA

Magee Rehabilitation Hospital, Philadelphia, PA

The Johns Hopkins Hospital, Baltimore, MD

Hahnemann Hospital, Philadelphia, PA

Hospital for Special Surgery, New York, NY

Burke Rehabilitation Center, White Plains, NY

And especially to all the first responders who always provide such quick and outstanding care

Thank you Emily C. Riley for your much needed editing skills!

*Thank you Jane Ramsey for the cover illustration that
so well captures our message.*

For further information, please contact:
RiseLikeThePhoenix.com